Sara Thurman

Small Beginnings
Companion Prayer Journal

Editor: Annie Laurie Ward

Publisher: Acts 1:8 Blessings

Paperback ISBN: 978-1-7341560-2-7
eBook ISBN: 978-1-7341560-3-4

Library of Congress Control Number: 2020920560

To Wayman
the strong, wise and gentle
wind beneath my wings whose memory
continues to be my voice of love

Contents

Introduction to Companion Prayer Journal

I did not think about the need for this companion journal when I wrote and released my book *Small Beginnings: A Journey to the Impossible* in 2019. However, over time I heard from my readers:

"I am writing all over the pages in my book."
"I need more space to write my thoughts."
"I answer the questions you ask in this book. It is like I am having a conversation with you."

Some of you are using this book in a group Bible study and have shared how nice it would be to have a companion journal to write, reflect, and create while reading the book.

So here I am at the starting line of another small beginning. Dear ones, I continually learn that this life we live truly is a series of small beginnings. As I write this companion journal, I am in the midst of grieving the passing of My Man. Wayman Lee Thurman, my husband and beloved companion, left this earth on January 19, 2020, with heart complications. I miss him like no one I have ever lost. He knew this journal was yet another small beginning for me. Living life without him is the most difficult small beginning I have ever experienced.

Day after day I am learning my new normal, like going to the grocery store without him, or coming home to an empty house. I've had to learn to grieve well and relearn daily living without my life companion by my side. Again, I have to set up the foundation of this new season with the plumb line of my life, Jesus. And He is faithful. Right now, while writing this *Small Beginnings Journal*, God has called me to create online Bible studies, a podcast called *Small Beginnings with Sara,* a book on grieving and a new paid membership group. Even in deep grief, I rejoice in the faithfulness of God and the joy of joining in the work that needs to begin. He knew this journal was another small beginning for me.

May this journal bless you. My prayer is that you will hear clearly from God as you meditate, reflect and consider the answers to these questions:

God, what do You want me to learn about You?

God, what do You want me to learn about myself?

God, what do You want me to learn in this moment on this journey with You?

Special Note to Reader: As you go through Small Beginnings you do not have to answer each question. Use these questions to connect to the heart of God. He wants to speak into your life and to be your guide and friend.

Reflections on the Introduction of Small Beginnings:

Oh God, hear our prayers. We yearn to know more of the intricacies of life in communion with all parts of You—Father God, Jesus Christ and Holy Spirit. Unveil Your mysteries to each of us in unique ways as we spend time with You. Help us find You, for You are waiting for us. You are at the beginning of the journey, at the end and everywhere in between. Oh, we love You, God. In Jesus' mighty name we pray, Amen!

"This book has your story in it, too. God wants to speak to your heart through the holy intersections of people I have met along the way…God wants to weave your story by using the first step of something that seems impossible, one thread at a time, choice by choice, intertwined with His never-ending grace and love, to create your tapestry." Page viii

- Have you ever considered your life as a tapestry? Ask God to show you His plans in the weaving. I pray He will show you His thread of gold as He weaves beauty and dreams into your story.
- Are you sensing something new in your life? In your relationship with God?
- What is God telling you about your "something impossible" right now? Write and/or draw your thoughts. Just start dreaming. You have permission from the God who gave you dreams.

Never doubt God's mighty power to work in you and accomplish all this. He will achieve infinitely more than your greatest request, your most unbelievable dream, and exceed your wildest imagination! He will outdo them all, for his miraculous power constantly energizes you. Ephesians 3:20 TPT

As you go through my book, may God open your ears to hear Him more clearly. May you stretch and grow all of your senses to know Jesus in greater ways as your Great Creator. Within this process of discovering more of God, He will receive more glory for His goodness.

chapter one

Your life is a series of small beginnings.

Dream the Impossible

Heavenly Father, we invite you to meet with us in this place and in this space of seeking You more. May it be more than we ever have experienced before. Show us the deep things of Your heart. Lord, we surrender all of ourselves to You as we lay down our own dreams and we desire to pick up Your dreams for us. You knew us in our mother's wombs; You knitted us so carefully together in Your image. Help us to reach our hands to You and open our hearts to You. You have more for us than we can dream or imagine. Almighty God, reveal to us Your secrets and Your dreams for our life. Show us our new small beginnings, for You are rejoicing to see the work begin. Give us vision in the places where we have not been able to believe the impossible, and that we would say 'No!" to our unbelief. Help our unbelief, God. We desire to dream the impossible with You, our Good Good Father who wants to give us all that You have. In Jesus' name, Amen!

Never doubt God's mighty power to work in you and accomplish all this. He will achieve infinitely more than your greatest request, your most unbelievable dream, and exceed your wildest imagination! He will outdo them all, for His miraculous power constantly energizes you!
Ephesians 3:20 TPT

Have you ever thought of your life as a series of small beginnings? Often times God uses our past experiences to help define our current realities. Write and/or draw some of your earliest memories of your own small beginnings.

Has God recently shown you new small beginnings? What examples are coming to your mind right now?

God wants to heal our past by bringing beauty from ashes. Ask God to show you areas of your life where you need to forgive others, and maybe even yourself. God redeems the things in the past to weave new and beautiful things for your present and future. Using the visual of a tapestry, ask God to show you how He has woven healing and freedom through your life. How has God used your past experiences to give freedom to someone else? Is He showing you a way He can do that now?

Draw or illustrate your current season of life as a beautiful tapestry. What will your current section include?

Have you ever asked God for His best and been willing to wait for it? Are you willing to do that today?.

Do you have a miracle story where God rescued you? Are you willing to tell your story as a testimony to others? Write and/or draw your miracle.

How Good Can God Be? Write a personal story of God's goodness in your own life.

"Deep grief requires holy comfort from above." This quote is so very poignant to my heart since Wayman passed. What have you lost that caused deep deep grief in your heart?

"How could I love Tuesday mornings and be so miserable in my thoughts? It was a battle of my mind. Who was I going to believe?" What is a current battle going on in your mind? Ask God to show you how to let Him be victorious in this battle.

When did you realize creating is a process of hanging out with God, not just making a finished product? Are you still discovering this mystery of how He created us to create? Has God surprised you in creating something you were not expecting?

My Suggestions

- Take time to reflect and pray and connect with God's impossible for your life. God tells us what to pray. *"And the Holy Spirit helps us in our weakness. For example, we don't know what God wants us to pray for. But the Holy Spirit prays for us with groaning that cannot be expressed in words."* Romans 8:26 NLT

- Believe!

- Pray for the impossible in agreement with God.

- Write it down, maybe in a journal or as a note. Write it in a place where you will see it again.

Reflections and Action Steps

- What dreams do you have that God has planted that many seem impossible?

- Be specific. Ask God for the prayers He wants you to pray in regard to your impossible dreams.

Lord, awaken Your dreams inside my heart and soul. Show me what to put on this page that will bless Your heart as I step into my new dreams, new small beginnings that connect me to Your heart. God, Thank You so much for going before me with every detail.

Use these pages to create a poem, a sketch or watercolor drawing of your dreams and visions from God at this point in your journey. Date it and name it. Push into areas that go past what you can dream or imagine on your own.

chapter
two

Our legacy is to pass on the beauty we create.

Pursue Purpose

Dear Jesus, we want what You want for us. We know You love each one of us. We are made in your image. Wow, God! We want to look more like You and act more like You in perfect love. Show us Your beautiful purposes for our life. Clean out the clutter and remove the noise that drowns out our purposes spoken to us from Your heart. We desire to have our prayers and our purpose be in perfect alignment with Your plans. Help us to surrender anything we hold onto in our lives that takes a place in front of You. Clean us up, dear God. Purify us to bring glory to Your name in all we think, all we do, and all we say. In the Mighty name of Jesus we pray. Amen!

For I know the plans I have for you," says the LORD. "They are plans for good and not for disaster, to give you a future and a hope." Jeremiah 29:11 NLT

"Everything rests on our purpose." In the small beginnings of your creative process do you have a focused purpose, or "your why"?

"When I attend to what God reveals, I am most blessed." What has God revealed to you most recently? Can you look back to the past few months, weeks or even days and see a new direction for your purpose?

God will always build on His Word. Do you have a life scripture or a scripture for this season? If not, ask God for one. Acts 1:8 has given me such direction and purpose.

God connected the parts of my life to be in alignment with His will. What a blessing of God's faithfulness to us! I am reminded of God's words to Joshua when he was leading the people after Moses died:

This is My command—be strong and courageous! Do not be afraid or discouraged for the Lord your God is with you wherever you go. Joshua 1:9 NLT

Can you see some places in your life where He is asking you to be strong and courageous? Do you believe God is with you in these new places?

"What seemed impossible was made possible because of the faithfulness of God."

Over and over I see God bringing the right people into my life to help me accomplish His works. Do you trust God to work out the details for you?

Are you listening for God's direction? Stop and ask Him specifically for the next step.

"The power of God's generosity intertwined with His purpose." Do you believe God to be a generous God? Write a testimony of your own experience of God's goodness. Then pray for God to show you an opportunity to share this testimony with someone else.

"God's amazing grace and purpose were ushered in through obedience that day." What has your experience been with being obedient when you hear clear direction from God?

"...portraying purpose beyond the physical canvas" Write an example of how God has worked in multiple levels beyond the physical aspects of your creative process.

Reflections and Action Steps

- Write your purpose statement for this season. In each season of life, our purposes may need realignment to God's purposes.

- Think about the three umbrellas: Loving God, Loving Ourselves, and Loving Others. Are there any action steps you need to take to be under the covering?

Lord, awaken Your dreams inside my heart and soul. Show me what to put on this page that will bless Your heart as I step into my new dreams, new small beginnings that connect me to Your heart. God, Thank You so much for going before me with every detail.

Use these pages to create a poem, a sketch or watercolor drawing of your dreams and visions from God at this point in your journey. Date it and name it. Push into areas that go past what you can dream or imagine on your own.

chapter
three

Do hard things.

Create Discipline

Oh Papa God, hear our cries for help with discipline. This is a really hard step for most of us. This requires action on our behavior and in our hearts. Holy Spirit, come and release self-control for us deep in our hearts. Let us have Your mind, the very mind of Christ, as we first discover the deeper plans You have for us. We want to go on the best path for us, dear God. Show us how to sow seeds that will grow deep roots and produce a harvest. Would You give us insight into our planting? Would You give us Your power and strength to take the next steps on our journey? Would you give us joy in this step of discipline? Jesus, could You show us immediate results in our obedience to Your directions? Help us keep our eyes on the goal of bringing You glory and praise in all we do. Thank You, God, for creating us with the ability to choose discipline. You made us with purpose and motivation. Fall on us anew, Holy Spirit, so that we may know we are in alignment with Your beautiful will for our lives. Yes, we can do hard things. In Jesus' mighty name, we pray. Amen!

"Create a new, clean heart, O God, and renew a right spirit within me."
Psalm 51:10 TPT

Our family of origin has an influence on us throughout our lives. What did your childhood teach you about discipline and what it is for?

Reframe any thoughts that discipline means punishment for a mistake. Think of it as training so that we have self control and obedience. Ask God to show you His heart behind discipline and its purpose. Obedience leads to God's face turning towards our own face. God always has purpose attached to discipline. What is His purpose for it in your life right now?

What aspects of discipline from your childhood influence your creativity? Is there room for more discipline?

Have you ever planted a garden? What did you learn from that experience?

"What is God doing today and how can I join in on the action?" This crucial question reframes our day to be kingdom focused. Answer the question and reflect on how to stay kingdom focused no matter what is in front of you. Readers, this could be a question you ask every day of your life.

Are you satisfied with your current level of self-control? What specific areas come to mind where you could use more Holy Spirit lead self control?

"My First 100 Day Project—A critical key to unlocking creativity through daily practice and discipline." Have you had a practice of daily creativity? If yes, how did the experience affect your creativity? If no, what would need to happen in your life to get in the habit of creating every day?

"Discipline is worth it when it is God inspired. He was inviting me into His project." Share about a time you know you were practicing God inspired discipline.

"Activate self-control to create the rhythms of discipline needed each day to reap the harvest and bring glory to God." Write a prayer below asking for this activation in your creative, physical, emotional, and spiritual life.

"Do not become dismayed at the baby steps and the small beginnings of each day." Name the places and spaces of the past where you have become dismayed. Now declare freedom in those places and ask God for His supernatural strength and help to overcome each step.

Reflections and Action Steps

- Reflect on a success in your past where you had the discipline to complete the task at hand. Celebrate your success.

- Think about a new area of your life where discipline can benefit your current situation. Can you take a step forward in discipline for five days? Ten days? Twenty days? Fifty days? One hundred days? Can you imagine your success of the completed goal?

Lord, awaken Your dreams inside my heart and soul. Show me what to put on this page that will bless Your heart as I step into my new dreams, new small beginnings that connect me to Your heart. God, Thank You so much for going before me with every detail.

Use these pages to create a poem, a sketch or watercolor drawing of your dreams and visions from God at this point in your journey. Date it and name it. Push into areas that go past what you can dream or imagine on your own.

chapter four

We need each other on this journey.

Find Your People

O Jesus, this step is such a gift from You. Show us our people. It is too hard to do this life without those You send to us as encouragers and helpers in times of need. If our circle of friends and family is small, Lord show us how to enlarge our circles, our tent stakes. Let us be brave and courageous and invite others into relationships. Lord God Almighty, I pray against offense and records of wrong. Would you help us clean the slates? Give us holy intersections with people to run with. Open doors to new healthy relationships. Help us show up for others in authentic and loving ways. Bless us with more friends and family who show Your patient and grace-filled love. Through Your blessing, we in turn bless You when we are in relationship with You and with others. In Jesus' holy name we pray. Amen!

Reflect on these two scriptures. This step is critical in moving forward in your relationships and loving those that God has placed in front of you. Are there any relationships, current or past, that need forgiveness or reconciliation? Ask God to help us forgive those who have wronged us. Ask God to give us the strength to ask someone for forgiveness if necessary. Then ask God to show you how to repair the broken walls of the past. Where does He want you to rebuild?

"[Love] is not irritable, and it keeps no record of being wronged."
I Corinthians 13:5 NLT

"If you are offering your gift at the altar and there remember that your brother or sister has something against you, leave your gift there in front of the altar. First go and be reconciled to them; then come and offer your gift."
Matthew 5:23 NIV

"This road is not meant to be a road traveled alone." Reflect on a time in your life where God sent you helpers along the way. Thank God for their help in time of need.

"My people make me better." Are you in a creative community? Ask God to help you get plugged in so that your confidence and skill level grow.

"*What factors influenced my shutdown?*" Do you ever have fear of failure over your creativity? Are there any external factors influencing your thoughts or creative space? Have you noticed a connection between feeling unsafe and the lack of flow in your thoughts and ideas?

"*I chose to believe the truth that I had the creative DNA from Jesus. He is the Great Creator and I am made in His image.*" Do you believe this truth? Have you ever believed the lie that you are not creative? Ask God to show you the lies of the past and speak the truth over your own unique creativity.

"Keep pouring out what He has given you and God will fill your cup to overflowing. Again. And again." Write down some specific times when God has used your creativity to bless others. Where does He want you to overflow today?

Reflections and Action Steps

- Write a list of your people. The people you can call in the middle of the night for difficult situations. The tribe who dances with you in those joyous celebrations.

- Now ask God to add to your tribe. Ask Him to show you the one in your community, your family, your social network who needs your care and attention. Reach beyond your own tent. Move out your tent stakes. Watch what God will do with your actions of love.

Lord, awaken Your dreams inside my heart and soul. Show me what to put on this page that will bless Your heart as I step into my new dreams, new small beginnings that connect me to Your heart. God, Thank You so much for going before me with every detail.

Use these pages to create a poem, a sketch or watercolor drawing of your dreams and visions from God at this point in your journey. Date it and name it. Push into areas that go past what you can dream or imagine on your own.

chapter
five

God is up to something in the detours.

Walk Out On The Water

God, my Father, thank You for trust. I trust You. I trust You. Yes, I trust You. You can see it all. God, You designed the blueprint of my life. Even though I have made decisions along my path that caused a few detours, here I stand. And I am grateful. Teach me to trust You even more. Let me know You are the One who sees me. You have not forgotten me. You will never leave my side. Your design for my life is beautiful. You don't waste any heartache or loss or brokenness. You are in charge. You are who I can trust. Every twist and turn can be used for beauty from the ashes. This is who You are; my God and my Savior is in all the details of my life. Thank You so much, Papa God, for caring for me and for helping me to be strong in You. I love You. I love You. I love You. It's You and me, Baby. We are on an adventure and I am not letting go of Your hand because I am walking on water to my Jesus. In Your name, Amen.

The Lord is my strength and shield. I trust Him with all my heart. He helps me, and my heart is filled with joy. I burst out in songs of thanksgiving.
Psalms 28:7 NLT

My inner dialogue continued, " Why do I put myself through this?" Have you asked yourself this same question after being defeated time and time again? Who is telling you that you are defeated? Who is your voice of reason?

""Come," Jesus said. So Peter gets out of the boat and begins to walk toward Jesus." Notice Peter did get out of the boat. He was walking on water. How are you walking on water? How are you doing the impossible?

"Once Peter is out on the water, he gets distracted." What are your distractions on your creative journey in this season?

"All the doubts and lies, they are like fiery arrows trying to find their way under my skin." The battle of your mind. Scripture tells us that there is a real battle going on:

> *Your hand-to-hand combat is not with human beings, but with the highest principalities and authorities operating in rebellion under the heavenly realms. For they are a powerful class of demon-gods and evil spirits that hold this dark world in bondage.* **Ephesians 6:12 TPT**

Who is winning in your life right now? What tools has God given us to fight?

> *Because of this, you must wear all the armor that God provides so you're protected as you confront the slanderer, for you are destined for all things and will rise victorious. Put on truth as a belt to strengthen you to stand in triumph. Put on holiness as the protective armor that covers your heart. Stand on your feet alert, then you'll always be ready to share the blessings of peace. In every battle, take faith as your wrap-around shield, for it is able to extinguish the blazing arrows coming at you from the Evil One! Embrace the power of salvation's full deliverance, like a helmet to protect your thoughts from lies. And take the mighty razor-sharp Spirit-sword of the spoken Word of God.* **Ephesians 6:13-18a TPT**

Take a moment to sketch what your tools and weapons of battle look like. How can you use each of these, through the power of Jesus, to win the battle of the mind that you are experiencing right now?

The Vision of Psalm 91. Has God shown you a vision to help you walk out on the water? Pray and ask God to increase your awareness of His presence in tangible ways.

"The young thief brought back the billfold and handed it to Wayman as we were standing in the circle." Have you been a witness to a miracle that would have been impossible if God had not intervened? Write down your testimony and declare that it is by the power of your testimony that more will come to know Him.

The intimacy of creating with God is described in Psalm 91:1-2 TPT *"When you sit enthroned under the shadow of Shaddai, you are hidden in the strength of God Most High. He's the hope that holds me and the Stronghold to shelter me, the only God for me, and my great confidence."* Our creativity is destined to collide with our intimacy with God when we commune with Him as we create. Have you experienced this safe place? Was it easier for you to create there?

"This time of intimacy with God was driving my creativity and moving me into a beautiful relationship." Is intimacy growing between you and your Creator?

"Perfectionism steals the joy in the journey of creating." Do you agree with this statement? Is it true for you? Has perfection ever served you well in the creative process?

"But yet, I still did not really believe I was an artist." This was the spring of 2016, about one and a half years after I started painting. Do you believe you are an artist/musician/writer/creative? What would need to be different for you to believe in your identity as a creative? Pray for your identity to line up with how God sees you. What does He say?

"Selling ourselves short because we think we are supposed to does not bring glory to Him. Listening to His voice and responding to obedience does." This is a critical point of victory. Listen to your self-talk. Are you negating the victory of Jesus in your life? Ask Jesus to open your ears to hear His truth. Do you speak negatively to yourself and your own creativity? What does your self-talk sound like? Declare victory in Jesus as a child of God who is created to create.

"The Etsy shop was a lesson in looking for the long lasting fruit." My Etsy shop had one sale. Have you felt defeated from spending hours and days and months preparing for a harvest that looks as if it isn't coming? This is when we ask God for specifics of His plans for us. Ask Him for clarity in the areas that are lacking long lasting fruit.

"Jesus is leading our dance." How are you doing letting Him lead? Do you know the steps? It takes trust and intimacy to dance well with a partner. Pray for an increase in trust, faith and intimacy as you continue to learn the steps and trust the One who is leading.

Reflections and Action Steps

- Reflect on the risks you've taken in your life. Have you taken any? Did you sink? Do you feel Jesus reaching to pull you up?

- What are you thinking about more—what you are afraid of or what you are dreaming of? Journal your thoughts.

- Practice saying affirmations based on Scripture out loud about who God says you are. Start believing the things that seem impossible.

Lord, awaken Your dreams inside my heart and soul. Show me what to put on this page that will bless Your heart as I step into my new dreams, new small beginnings that connect me to Your heart. God, Thank You so much for going before me with every detail.

Use these pages to create a poem, a sketch or watercolor drawing of your dreams and visions from God at this point in your journey. Date it and name it. Push into areas that go past what you can dream or imagine on your own.

chapter
six

God hasn't ever not been talking.

Keep Your Eyes Open

Heavenly Father, we invite You into this time of self discovery and creativity. As this reader moves through this chapter, I pray You make one thing very clear: You are always speaking, but not always in a way that we are expecting. You always speak through Your written word, sometimes You speak audibly, sometimes You speak to our very hearts, and sometimes You speak through a friend. You have spoken to me through the trees blowing in the wind, the giggles of my granddaughters, the smell of wildflowers, the taste of an amazing meal, the gentle touch of my husband's hand on my shoulder. You gave us these five senses to not only enjoy this life You have given us, but to enjoy true communion with you. Sometimes it feels like You are silent and far away. Even though we may know in our heads that it isn't true, remind us to go to those places where we can find You again; scripture, stillness, nature, a wise friend. We don't want to just learn how to look for You with our eyes, but with all of our senses. You created us with all five senses to grasp Your great love for us. And I pray that each reader can grasp in a new way that we can, at any moment, take how You creatively communicate and use it to create beauty ourselves. We are so grateful. In Jesus' name, Amen!

The Lord went ahead of them. He guided them during the day with a pillar of cloud, and He provided light at night with a pillar of fire. This allowed them to travel by day or by night. And the Lord did not remove the pillar of cloud or pillar of fire from its place in front of the people.
Exodus 13:21-22

God's people in Exodus never had to wonder if there were going the right way. God is going before you. You have to look up. God is our Guide and our Light.

Have you ever heard God's voice through another person or an angel? Sometimes God uses angels to talk to His children.

If you own a business with your spouse, what has it been like? What are some of the advantages and disadvantages? Are there areas God would want you to expand or improve upon?

"It takes discipline and practice to make sure my eyes and ears are open to what the Lord has for me." What does this mean to you? Use all five senses to listen and seek direction God has for you. What is He showing you right now at this moment through your five senses?

God restored my actions when I did not respond in a timely manner with Natasha's request for an angel. He brought forth many ripple effects with the angel I painted and named after her. Write about a time God brought restoration beyond your own expectations when you fell short. What is happening right now in your life where you need God to come and do the same?

"He is speaking. Will I keep listening?" Tell about a time when you heard God's voice and He unveiled His beauty and purposes before you.

Reflections and Action Steps

- Think about a time you heard God give you a direction in your life. Celebrate His voice in your life.

- Ask for more encounters with God's voice. Ask Him to speak into your life. Take note of the sacred experience.

Lord, awaken Your dreams inside my heart and soul. Show me what to put on this page that will bless Your heart as I step into my new dreams, new small beginnings that connect me to Your heart. God, Thank You so much for going before me with every detail.

Use these pages to create a poem, a sketch or watercolor drawing of your dreams and visions from God at this point in your journey. Date it and name it. Push into areas that go past what you can dream or imagine on your own.

chapter
seven

God is never going to run out of creativity.

Stick With Your Passion

Oh, dear Creator, You've placed a creative passion inside each of us. It is part of our DNA because we have You inside of us. I don't want to stop when things get difficult. I want Your passion to flow through me and give me the boost to push through the heartache, the pain, the disappointment, the grief, the loss, the rejection, and the list goes on. Bring me to the other side of my pain. Jesus, You went to the cross so mankind could be saved from eternal death and be given the gift of eternal life. This is the ultimate example and gift to us. Infuse us, Dear Jesus, with strength when we are weak, weary, overwhelmed and burdened. Infuse us with supernatural

I pray that your hearts will be flooded with light so that you can understand the confident hope HE has given to those He called — His holy people who are His rich and glorious inheritance.
Ephesians 1:18 NLT

understanding that this battle is Yours and not ours. On top of which, the battle was over and finished on the cross. We only need to accept this freedom and grace. You already have victory. You are our Victorious God. We are Your beautiful children who receive our rich inheritance. So of course, we have to keep going bravely on the pathway You have placed in front of us. Let us see the victory line. Let us hear You and the great cloud of witnesses cheering us onward. Let us taste Your goodness this side of heaven while we join in bringing Your Kingdom to Earth. Let us feel Your touch and embrace in such a way that we know we are in Your presence. Jesus, You are our Passion. We are not giving up nor give in. We are pressing onward and upward until we see You face to face. In Jesus' name we pray, Amen.

Have you ever considered your creativity as worship to God? Consider the process of painting as an analogy to worshiping God: the image is Christ, the mood is the spirit of worship, and texture is changed lives. Each layer and each stroke is part of worship. How can you compare your worship to your creativity?

"Pursuing excellence leaves room for growth and honing a skill, while not expecting perfection." What do you think is the difference between excellence and perfection?

"I learned in this journey to trust when I hear God speak to me." Do you trust God in new circumstances?

Is it fairly easy for you to stop pursuing your passion? Know there will be roadblocks along the way. Are you willing to push through those obstacles?

God can use surprise friendships and relationships to add fuel and new bursts of energy to your creative journey. Has God ever given you a surprising relationship just when you needed it?

We know God is up to something when peace and joy accompany new things. There is so much joy when God awakens new desires and passions. Ask God to awaken any dormant passions that He wants you to walk toward in this season. Is there something specific that you feel stirring inside you?

Reflections and Action Steps

- Reflect on your top three passions in life. Look for the thread of God's direction interwoven with these passions. Can you see it?

- Ask God for the next steps to expand your passions to the new places He wants to use the gifts He has given you.

Lord, awaken Your dreams inside my heart and soul. Show me what to put on this page that will bless Your heart as I step into my new dreams, new small beginnings that connect me to Your heart. God, Thank You so much for going before me with every detail.

Use these pages to create a poem, a sketch or watercolor drawing of your dreams and visions from God at this point in your journey. Date it and name it. Push into areas that go past what you can dream or imagine on your own.

chapter eight

God knows what is underneath. You are safe.

Balance the Layers

Dear Lord Jesus, oh how we need You to be Lord over every aspect of our existence. Will you take us to a new place spiritually so we can see Your plans more clearly? We can get really off balance when things do not go the way we think they should. Come into our time and into our seasons of life. Come into our waiting. Come into the rhythms of our days and our nights. We like to decide what is best. We want things to speed up, slow down, stop and rewind all in one breath. We are easily discontent when we are without You. Lord Jesus, may we surrender all of our time and our earthly experiences this side of heaven. You, Great I Am, know all things. You can see it all. Your love for us is full of wisdom and truth. May we surrender all parts of our lives to You, the physical, emotional and spiritual. Show us and teach us how to balance all the layers so that we trust You with all circumstances. In Jesus' name we pray, Amen.

"Relationships for the win." What does that statement mean to you? Are your priorities in alignment with what you are hearing from God?

> *"For I know the plans I have for you,"* says the Lord. *"They are plans for good and not for disaster, to give you a future and hope."*
> Jeremiah 29:11 NLT

"It was not about the art." This statement seems confusing. Isn't this a book about art? What are your thoughts about my statement? If it's not about the art, then what is "it" about?

"Our rear guard is His glory. The ripple effects of His love are never ending."

Then your salvation will come like the dawn, and your wound will quickly heal. Your godliness will lead you forward, and the glory of the Lord will protect you from behind. Isaiah 58:8 NLT

Do you believe what God says in Isaiah 58:8? Does God go before us and behind us on this journey? Write an example of God moving before or after a situation.

"Be aware of what God is saying as you practice. How does it make you feel? What makes your work unique? We are not just to copy another's work. We get to allow God's DNA within each of us to come out as our own personal trademark." How does it make you feel? What makes your work unique?

"As I started to honor my space at home, I also began to honor my art." Do you have a dedicated space to be creative? Does it need some attention?

"But if my joy is dependent on the big sale, then my heart is entirely in the wrong place." What role do sales or success play in shaping your identity as an artist or creative?

"God sent me specific people, once again, who needed to experience His unfailing love. How easy it is for me to forget my purpose." Do you know your purpose when creating? Are you centering on that purpose daily?

"Thy Kingdom Come, Thy Will Be Done" painting was a bridge to reconciliation. How is God using you to bring reconciliation in broken relationships?

"I have had to establish healthy rhythms of balance in the process of becoming an artist. Should this be a business or a ministry? God has shown me the beautiful balance of ministry and business side by side." Are you struggling to balance priorities in your creative journey right now? Pray and ask God for clarity for the season.

Reflections and Action Steps

- How is it going with all the parts of our life—business, spiritual, emotional, physical? Is one draining your cup more than others?

- Think about the next three months of your life. Does anything need to be adjusted to get in better alignment to balance in your life?

Lord, awaken Your dreams inside my heart and soul. Show me what to put on this page that will bless Your heart as I step into my new dreams, new small beginnings that connect me to Your heart. God, Thank You so much for going before me with every detail.

Use these pages to create a poem, a sketch or watercolor drawing of your dreams and visions from God at this point in your journey. Date it and name it. Push into areas that go past what you can dream or imagine on your own.

chapter
nine

We are the story for all eternity.

Document the Journey

Oh, Jesus, our lives are telling Your story of eternal love. Let us embrace our unique stories. Let us speak of Your goodness in the land of the living. Let us tell our stories so Your name will be made famous throughout the earth. Show us the gold thread in the tapestry of our lives - the faithfulness and love you have for Your people. You created us to tell Your story of love. Awaken us, God Almighty, to write our stories with You as the main golden thread of hope and love. Give us Your eyes to see the gold in our lives. Thank You for creating us in Your image, breathing the breath of life into our lungs. Help us to document our journeys well, with You at the center of our stories. In Jesus name we pray, Amen.

Yet I am confident I will see the Lord's goodness while I am here in the Land of the Living.
Psalm 27:13 NLT

"How can we be sure to remember what God has done? Document the journey." Are you documenting your journey? Do you need to start a journal?

"God loves stories." Do you believe He loves your story? What beautiful things has He shown you about your own story?

The painting called "I Will Leave This House Singing" represents a moment that I will never forget. God, please show us more holy intersections. Have you experienced a holy intersection with someone, maybe even a complete stranger?

"When I started this process, I was totally unaware of the power of spoken words over my life." Then God set me straight about Spoken Words. *"Instead, I bring them to God, write them down, repeat them and believe that they are a part of my destiny and legacy."* How have words spoken over you affected your life? Ask God for more words of life to be spoken over you and your creative journey.

"I know God sets up holy intersections time after time with my art and my story of the impossible." Has God used something you have created as a turning point in someone else's life? Has God used something that someone else has created as a turning point in your own life?

Reflections and Action Steps

• We cannot be the overflow and tell our story unless we are healed and filled up by God. What step do you need to take to document your own story? Who are you sharing your story with?

• Think about others God has put in your path that need to hear your story. Think big! Take a step forward to make it happen. Is it a book? A blog? A piece of art? A cup of coffee with a new friend?

Lord, awaken Your dreams inside my heart and soul. Show me what to put on this page that will bless Your heart as I step into my new dreams, new small beginnings that connect me to Your heart. God, Thank You so much for going before me with every detail.

Use these pages to create a poem, a sketch or watercolor drawing of your dreams and visions from God at this point in your journey. Date it and name it. Push into areas that go past what you can dream or imagine on your own.

chapter
ten

We are never finished, always in process.

Hold it all Lightly

God, our Father, You see it all. You see what we can't yet see. Will You give us Your eyes? Will You help us see Your love? Thank you, Papa God. Help us to be good stewards of all You have gifted us this side of heaven. Help us be thankful for the simple yet profound things in our lives. Help us appreciate the plate You are serving us today. May we taste and see how good You are as our Bread of Life. May we drink deeply of Your cup. May we not rush through life, but savor the holy moments of just being with You- communing with our Great Creator on a nature walk, painting a picture, taking a picture, preparing a meal for our family, laughing with a friend, playing with a baby, watching the sunrise, and on and on. Help us to fully lay down all the things we are holding on to. You, O God know what to give us and what to take. You can be trusted, for You are God Almighty. You gave Your son unto death so we can live forever with You. Help us hold this journey lightly, with our eyes and hearts on the grand prize of eternal life with You. In Jesus' name, Amen.

"Never doubt God's mighty power to work in you and accomplish all this. He will achieve infinitely more than your greatest request, your most unbelievable dream, and exceed your wildest imagination! He will outdo them all, for this miraculous power constantly energizes you."
Ephesians 3:20 TPT

When you read the scripture above do you really believe that God's mighty power is at work within you? Tell God how you feel about this truth.

God always has a plan. You cannot always see every step, but you can trust God in making sure He has gone before you. In my story about painting "You Are My Delight", it was clear God had gone before me my very first night painting at Bethel Austin Church. Write about a time in your life when you knew God had gone before you.

The prodigal son's story has some deep layers. Think about the angry older brother who would not celebrate the homecoming of his younger brother. Ask God to reveal any jealous or comparing thoughts to others. Think about your family, the creative realm, FaceBook, Instagram or other social media. Repent and pull out that anger and jealousy. Ask God to show the root of this sin. Write about your next steps in rooting out these thorns.

"…everything I have is yours." Luke 15:31 NLT- The Father is telling the older son this truth. Do you believe that everything the Father has is yours? It is critical in your journey as a creative and child of God to believe and accept the Father's words. It changes everything and allows us to flow in joy and strength of our unique abilities. We do not need to be angry about someone else having more than us. Be willing to go deep with God in this area. What is God telling you about believing what He says? What does it look like for you to accept that everything He has is yours?

Will you celebrate your own small beginnings? Peter had to first believe he could walk on water or he would not have even put one foot out of the boat. He believed and then stepped out of the boat and walked on water. Will you believe and trust in the Creator God for the next step?

Reflections and Action Steps

- What is next in your journey? What is the next small step to your impossible? Can you take the next step?

- Write down an impossible prayer that God has put on your heart. A prayer that when it is answered only God could have answered it.

Lord, awaken Your dreams inside my heart and soul. Show me what to put on this page that will bless Your heart as I step into my new dreams, new small beginnings that connect me to Your heart. God, Thank You so much for going before me with every detail.

Use these pages to create a poem, a sketch or watercolor drawing of your dreams and visions from God at this point in your journey. Date it and name it. Push into areas that go past what you can dream or imagine on your own.

Acknowledgments

Thank you to My Man who lived my book *Small Beginnings: A Journey to the Impossible.* When I asked him if he had read my book, he replied with a big grin on his face, "I have lived your book, I don't need to read it." Such a true response. Wayman Lee Thurman lived side by side with me on this journey. We never dreamed that *Small Beginnings* would have such a positive impact on the world. He listened to me as I read him the different pieces of this tapestry, our story woven together by God's love and grace. As I spent 11 months writing, Wayman listened to me read aloud the many vignettes and watched as God showed more and more people His love for them through the paint at the end of my paintbrush.

God gives me strength each day to take the next step. As I reread *Small Beginnings* in preparing this journal, I see the wisdom of My Man still having ripple effects on my life, the life of anyone who reads this book, and into eternity.

Keep up to date with Sara's forthcoming published works,
artwork and courses by visiting www.SaraThurman.com.

A review of the Small Beginnings Companion Prayer Journal
is encouraged and appreciated.

Join Sara on social media to connect with her
and God and to find your purpose.
https://www.instagram.com/actsoneeightblessings/
https://www.facebook.com/actsoneeightblessings

Made in the USA
Columbia, SC
27 February 2021